DAILY JOY

Photos and Wisdom to Lift Your Spirit

DAILY JOY

Photos and Wisdom to Lift Your Spirit

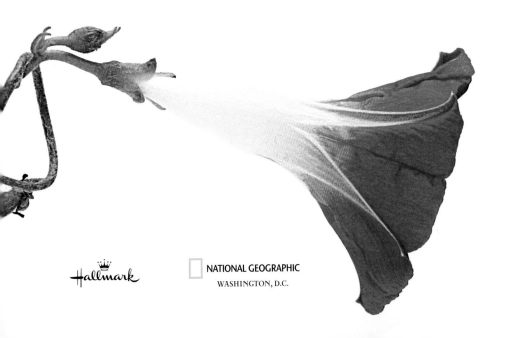

Hallmark

☐ NATIONAL GEOGRAPHIC

WASHINGTON, D.C.

Published in 2014 by Hallmark Gift Books, a division of Hallmark Cards, Inc., in cooperation with National Geographic Society.

Copyright © 2012 National Geographic Society

This edition published in 2013 by Hallmark Gift Books, a division of Hallmark Cards, Inc., Kansas City, MO 64141 under license from the National Geographic Society. Visit us on the Web at Hallmark.com.

Cover image and design: Image Plan/Corbis, Jonathan Halling
Interior design: Cinda Rose

ISBN: 978-1-59530-657-9
BOK1295

Printed and bound in China

A Gift For:

_____

From:

_____

We must be willing
to get rid of the life
we've planned,
so as to have the life
that is waiting for us.

~ Joseph Campbell

There is only one journey:
going inside yourself.

~ Rainer Maria Rilke

DAY 3

The future belongs to those who believe
in the beauty of their dreams.

~ Eleanor Roosevelt

DAY 4

What lies behind us
and what lies before us
are small matters
compared to what lies
within us.

~ Ralph Waldo Emerson

DAY 5

The mind is not a vessel to be filled,
but a fire to be kindled.

~ Plutarch

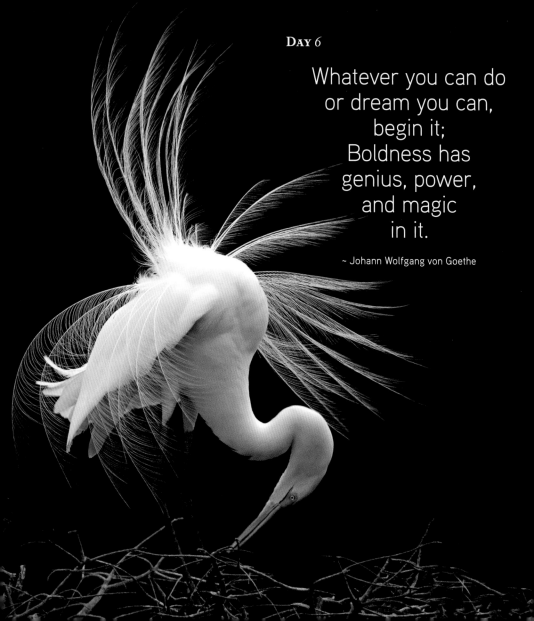

DAY 6

Whatever you can do
or dream you can,
begin it;
Boldness has
genius, power,
and magic
in it.

~ Johann Wolfgang von Goethe

Without forgiveness, there is no future.

~ Desmond Tutu

DAY 8

Dreams come true; without that possibility,
nature would not incite us to have them.

~ John Updike

DAY 9

Logic will get you from A to B.
Imagination will take you everywhere.

~ Albert Einstein

Above all, watch with glittering eyes
the whole world around you because
the greatest secrets are always
hidden in the most unlikely places.
Those who don't believe in magic
will never find it.

~ Roald Dahl

Joy is what happens to us
when we allow ourselves to recognize
how good things really are.

~ Marianne Williamson

Every great dream begins with a dreamer.
Always remember, you have within you
the strength, the patience, and the passion
to reach for the stars
to change the world.

~ Harriet Tubman

Only passions, great passions,
can elevate the soul to great things.

~ Denis Diderot

March on. Do not tarry. To go forward is
to move toward perfection. March on, and fear not
the thorns, or the sharp stones on life's path.

~ Kahlil Gibran

DAY *15*

Our aspirations are our possibilities.

~ Samuel Johnson

In the depth of winter
I finally learned
that there was in me
an invincible summer.

~ Albert Camus

Who, being loved, is poor?

~ Oscar Wilde

DAY *18*

Being deeply loved by someone
gives you strength,
while loving someone deeply
gives you courage.

~ Lao-tzu

Love does not consist
in gazing at each other,
but in looking outward together
in the same direction.

~ Antoine de Saint-Exupéry

Day 20

Each friend represents a world in us,
a world possibly not born until they arrive.
And it is only by this meeting
that a new world is born.

~ Anaïs Nin

मुबारक
...त परिवार
हार्दिक
भारत I Love

I LOVE YOU

DAY *21*

Forgiveness
is the final form
of love.

~ Reinhold Niebuhr

The summit of happiness is reached
when a person is ready to be
what he is.

~ Desiderius Erasmus

DAY *23*

It is only with the heart
that one can see rightly;
what is essential
is invisible to the eye.

~ Antoine de Saint-Exupéry

DAY 24

Only the heart
knows how
to find
what is precious.

~ Fyodor Dostoyevsky

Things do not change;
we change.

~ Henry David Thoreau

The one thing
we can never get
enough of
is love.
And the one thing
we never give
enough of
is love.

~ Henry Miller

DAY 27

Let there be no purpose
in friendship
save the deepening
of the spirit.

~ Kahlil Gibran

What is passion?
It is surely
the becoming of a person.

~ John Boorman

DAY *29*

Realize deeply
that the present moment
is all you ever have.

~ Eckhart Tolle

We make a living by what
we get. We make a life by
what we give.

~ Sir Winston Churchill

When you
do things
from your soul,
you feel a river
moving in you,
a joy.

~ Rumi

Happiness is when
what you think,
what you say, and
what you do
are in harmony.

~ Mohandas Gandhi

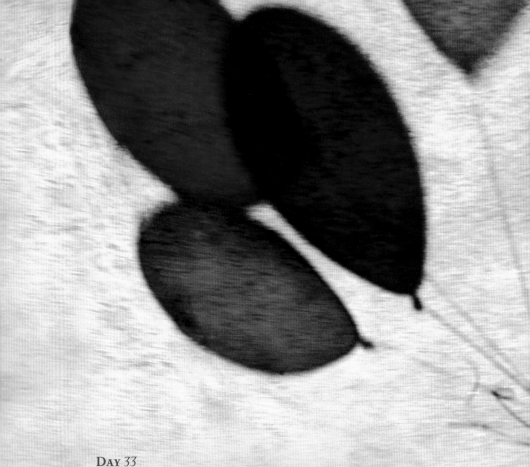

DAY 33

If you have nothing at all to create,
then perhaps you create yourself.

~ Carl Jung

DAY 34

Everything
in the universe
is within you.
Ask all from
yourself.

~ Rumi

DAY 35

Everyone thinks
of changing the world,
but no one thinks
of changing himself.

~ Leo Tolstoy

What we have once enjoyed,
we can never lose.
All that we love deeply
becomes a part of us.

~ Helen Keller

The privilege
of a lifetime
is being
who you are.

~ Joseph Campbell

The shoe that fits one person
pinches another;
there is no recipe for living
that suits all cases.

~ Carl Jung

Adopt the pace of nature;
her secret is patience.

~ Ralph Waldo Emerson

DAY 40

To be nobody but yourself
in a world
which is doing its best,
night and day,
to make you everybody else
means to fight
the hardest battle
which any human being
can fight.
Never stop fighting.

~ e. e. cummings

My favorite thing
is to go where
I've never been.

~ Diane Arbus

You are built not to shrink down to less,
but to blossom into more.
To be more splendid.
To be more extraordinary.
To use every moment to fill yourself up.

~ Oprah Winfrey

I have learned that success
is to be measured not so much
by the position that one has reached in life
as by the obstacles which he has overcome
while trying to succeed.

~ Booker T. Washington

It is impossible
to live without failing
at something—
unless you live
so cautiously
that you might as well
not have lived at all,
in which case
you have failed
by default.

~ J. K. Rowling

Trust yourself.
You know more than you think you do.

~ Benjamin Spock

Because things are
the way they are,
things will not stay
the way they are.

~Bertolt Brecht

It isn't where you came from,
it's where you're going that counts.

~ Ella Fitzgerald

DAY 48

Opportunities
are usually disguised
as hard work,
so most people
don't recognize them.

~ Ann Landers

Live out of
your imagination,
not your history.

~ Arthur Bryan

DAY *50*

If we don't change,
we don't grow.
If we don't grow,
we aren't really living.

~ Gail Sheehy

Real courage is when you know
you're licked before you begin—
but you begin anyway
and see it through no matter what.

~ Harper Lee

Nurture your mind
with great thoughts,
for you will never
go any higher
than you think.

~ Benjamin Disraeli

DAY *53*

Always remember the future
comes one day at a time.

~ Dean Acheson

DAY *54*

I'm not afraid of storms,
for I'm learning how to sail my ship.

~ Louisa May Alcott

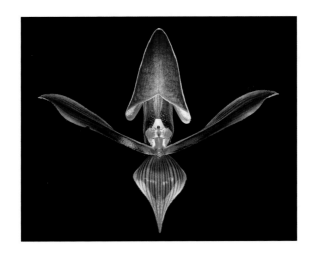

Fortune favors the bold.

~ Virgil

Courage
is resistance
to fear,
mastery of fear—
but not absence
of fear.

~ Mark Twain

Inside myself is a place
where I live all alone.
That's where you renew
your springs
that never dry up.

~ Pearl S. Buck

Life is a series of collisions with the future.

~ José Ortega y Gasset

Courage is what it takes to stand up
and speak; courage is also what it takes
to sit down and listen.

~ Sir Winston Churchill

DAY 60

The weak
can never forgive.
Forgiveness is
the attribute of
the strong.

~ Mohandas Gandhi

True bravery is shown
by performing without witness
what one might be capable
of doing before all the world.

~ François de la Rochefoucauld

When in doubt,
tell the truth.

~ Mark Twain

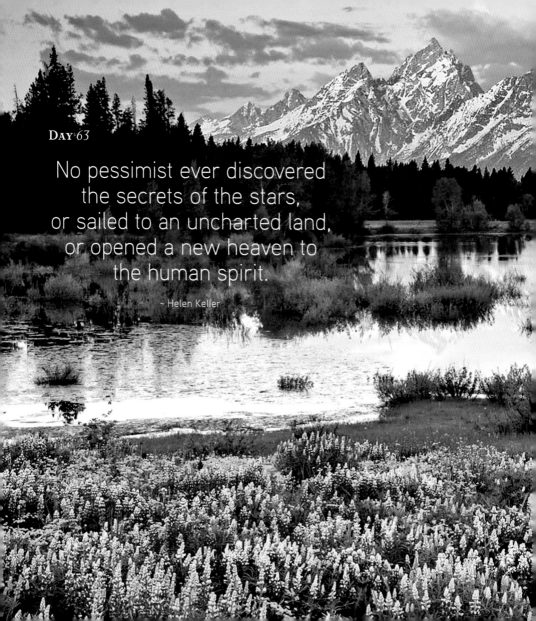

DAY 63

No pessimist ever discovered
the secrets of the stars,
or sailed to an uncharted land,
or opened a new heaven to
the human spirit.

~ Helen Keller

I never lose sight
of the fact
that just being is fun.

~ Katharine Hepburn

DAY 65

Turn your wounds
into wisdom.

~ Oprah Winfrey

There are years
that ask questions,
and years that answer.

~ Zora Neale Hurston

Look at everything
as though you were seeing it
for either the first or last time.
Then your time on earth
will be filled with glory.

~ Betty Smith

One is never
fortunate
or as unfortunate
as one imagines.

~ François de la Rochefoucauld

We can always choose
to perceive things differently.
You can focus on
what's wrong in your life,
or you can focus on
what's right.

~ Marianne Williamson

God gave us our memories
that we might have roses in December.

~ J. M. Barrie

The voyage
of discovery is not
in seeking
new landscapes,
but in having
new eyes.

~ Marcel Proust

Look deep into nature, and then you
will understand everything better.

~ Albert Einstein

DAY 73

It does not do
to dwell on dreams
and forget to live.

~ J. K. Rowling

Happiness is largely
an attitude of mind, of viewing life
from the right angle.

~ Dale Carnegie

To be able to look back upon
one's life in satisfaction
is to live twice.

~ Kahlil Gibran

The years teach much
which the days never knew.

~ Ralph Waldo Emerson

Pleasure is very seldom found
where it is sought.
Our brightest blazes
are commonly kindled by
unexpected sparks.

~ Samuel Johnson

DAY 78

Life was not meant to be easy,
but take courage: it can be delightful.

~ George Bernard Shaw

If you wait for
the perfect moment
when all is safe
and assured,
it may never arrive.
Mountains will not
be climbed,
races won,
or lasting happiness
achieved.

~ Maurice Chevalier

DAY *80*

What we play is life.

~ Louis Armstrong

Today a new sun rises for me;
everything lives,
everything is animated,
everything seems to speak to me
of my passion,
everything invites me to cherish it.

~ Ninon de Lenclos

DAY 82

Only those who risk going too
far can possibly find out
how far one can go.

~ T. S. Eliot

The young
do not know enough
to be prudent and
therefore they
attempt
the impossible—
and achieve it,
generation after
generation.

~ Pearl S. Buck

All life is an experiment.
The more experiments you make,
the better.

~ Ralph Waldo Emerson

DAY *85*

The most exciting happiness
is happiness generated by forces
beyond your control.

~ Ogden Nash

The harder the conflict,
the more glorious
the triumph.

~ Thomas Paine

Life itself
is the most wonderful fairy tale.

~ Hans Christian Andersen

Nobody can conceive
or imagine all the wonders
there are unseen and
unseeable in the world.

~ Francis P. Church

Throw your dream into space
like a kite, and you do not know
what it will bring back:
a new life, a new friend,
a new love,
a new country.

~ Anaïs Nin

Be bold . . .
When you embark
for strange places,
don't leave
any of yourself
safely on shore.

~ Alan Alda

Though we travel the world over
to find the beautiful, we must carry it
with us or we find it not.

~ Ralph Waldo Emerson

The soul should always
stand ajar,
ready to welcome
the ecstatic experience.

~ Emily Dickinson

Life calls the tune, we dance.

~ John Galsworthy

DAY 94

Stay hungry.
Stay foolish.

~ Steve Jobs

Stuff your eyes with wonder;
live as if you'd drop dead in ten seconds.
See the world. It's more fantastic than
any dream made or paid for in factories.

~ Ray Bradbury

There are only two ways
to live your life.
One is as though
nothing is a miracle.
The other
is as though everything
is a miracle.

~ Albert Einstein

If you can spend a perfectly useless afternoon in a perfectly useless manner, you have learned how to live.

~ Lin Yutang

The real happiness of life is to enjoy the present,
without any anxious dependence upon the future.

~ Lucius Annaeus Seneca

If you obey
all the rules
you miss
all the fun.

~ Katharine Hepburn

The power of imagination
makes us infinite.

~ John Muir

Freedom lies in being bold.

~ Robert Frost

Day 102

Lock up your libraries if you like, but there is
no gate, no lock, no bolt, that you can set upon
the freedom of my mind.

~ Virginia Woolf

To have
what we want
is riches;
but to be able to
do without
is power.

~ George Macdonald

We do not need magic
to change the world,
we carry all the power we need
inside ourselves already:
we have the power
to imagine better.

~ J. K. Rowling

Try again. Fail again. Fail better.

~ Samuel Beckett

Perhaps
loving something
is the only
starting place there is
for making your life
your own.

~ Alice Koller

Learn to get in touch with the silence
within yourself and know that everything
in this life has a purpose.

~ Elisabeth Kübler-Ross

DAY *108*

Success is often achieved by those who
don't know that failure is inevitable.

~ Coco Chanel

Day *109*

Don't find fault; find a remedy.

~ Henry Ford

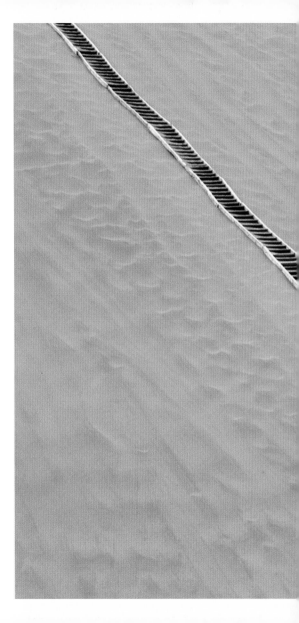

Inspiration
usually comes
during work,
rather than
before it.

~ Madeleine L'Engle

Don't aim for success if you want it;
just do what you love and believe in,
and it will come naturally.

~ David Frost

Pleasure and action
make the hours seem short.

~ William Shakespeare

DAY *113*

Resolve to keep happy,
and your joy and you shall form
an invincible host against difficulties.

~ Helen Keller

Nothing is a waste of time
if you use the experience wisely.

~ Auguste Rodin

Day *115*

To succeed in life, you need two things:
ignorance and confidence.

~ Mark Twain

DAY *116*

Failure is only the opportunity to
begin again more intelligently.

~ Henry Ford

Out of clutter,
find simplicity.

~ Albert Einstein

DAY *118*

With the new day comes new strength
and new thoughts.

~ Eleanor Roosevelt

Success consists of going
from failure to failure
without loss of enthusiasm.

~ Sir Winston Churchill

Let us be grateful to people
who make us happy;
they are the charming gardeners
who make our souls blossom.

~ Marcel Proust

The purpose
of life
is a life of
purpose.

~ Robert Byrne

One of the secrets
of a happy life
is continuous
small treats.

~ Iris Murdoch

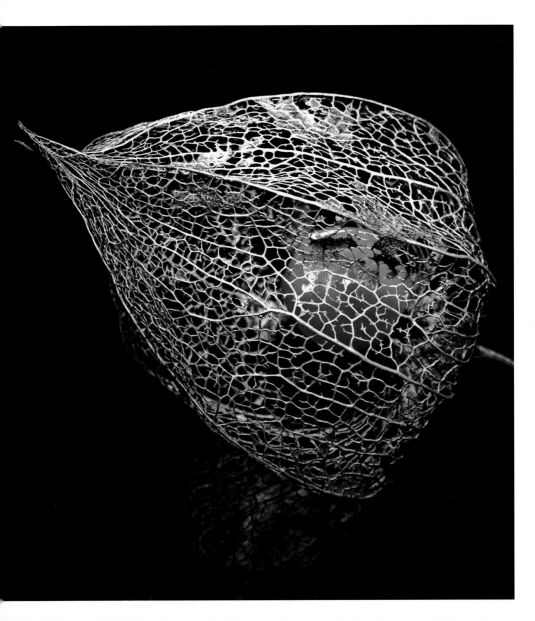

Those who
bring sunshine
to the lives of others
cannot keep it from
themselves.

~ J. M. Barrie

Now and then it's good to pause
in our pursuit of happiness
and just be happy.

~ Guillaume Apollinaire

If only we'd stop trying
to be happy we'd have
a pretty good time.

~ Edith Wharton

The grand essentials of happiness are:
something to do, something to love,
and something to hope for.

~ Alexander Chalmers

If you always do
what interests you,
at least one person
is pleased.

~ Katharine Hepburn

If you find it in your heart to care for
somebody else,
you will have succeeded.

~ Maya Angelou

To find out what one is fitted to do,
and to secure an opportunity to do it,
is the key to happiness.

~ John Dewey

The best way to cheer yourself up is
to try to cheer somebody else up.

~ Mark Twain

One cannot collect
all the beautiful shells on the beach.
One can collect only a few,
and they are more beautiful
if they are few.

~ Anne Morrow Lindbergh

True happiness consists
not in the multitude of friends,
but in the worth and choice.

~ Ben Jonson

Anything you're good at
contributes to happiness.

~ Bertrand Russell

When what we are is
what we want to be,
that's happiness.

~ Malcolm Forbes

It is easy to be heavy;
it is hard to be light.

~ G. K. Chesterton

Don't wait around
for other people
to be happy for you.
Any happiness
you get,
you've got to
make yourself.

~ Alice Walker

The art of being wise
is the art of knowing what to overlook.

~ William James

Holding on to anger is like
grasping a hot coal
with the intent of throwing it
at someone else;
you are the one who gets burned.

~ Buddha

You can catch health,
happiness, and success
from others
just as easily as
you can catch worries,
bitterness, and failure.

~ Dale Carnegie

Not everything that can be counted
counts, and not everything that
counts can be counted.

~ Albert Einstein

Don't grieve.
Anything you lose
comes round
in another form.

~ Rumi

The most common
way people give up
their power is
by thinking
they don't have any.

~ Alice Walker

The person who has lived the most
is not the one with the most years
but the one with
the richest experiences.

~ Jean-Jacques Rosseau

Whoever is careless with truth
in small matters cannot be trusted
in important affairs.

~ Albert Einstein

DAY *145*

Our perfect companions
never have fewer than four feet.

~ Colette

Things are always in transition.
Nothing ever sums itself up
in the way that we like to
dream about.

~ Pema Chödrön

Happiness often sneaks in
through a door you didn't know
you left open.

~ John Barrymore

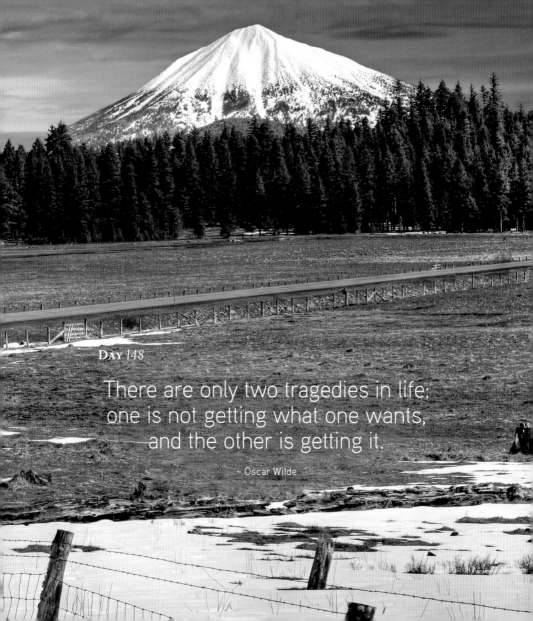

DAY *148*

There are only two tragedies in life:
one is not getting what one wants,
and the other is getting it.

~ Oscar Wilde

The body is a sacred garment.
It's your first and last garment;
it is what you enter life in and
what you depart life with,
and it should be treated
with honor.

~ Martha Graham

DAY *150*

The human race has one really effective
weapon, and that is laughter.

~ Mark Twain

Instead of comparing
our lot with that
of those who are
more fortunate
than we are, we
should compare it
with the lot
of the great majority
of our fellow men.
It then appears that
we are among
the privileged.

~ Helen Keller

DAY 152

Forgiveness is a funny thing.
It warms the heart and
cools the sting.

~ William Arthur Ward

Your successes and happiness
are forgiven you
only if you generously consent
to share them.

~ Albert Camus

It is good to have an end to journey
toward; but it is the journey
that matters, in the end.

~ Ursula K. Le Guin

DAY *155*

Don't worry about losing. If it is right,
it happens—the main thing is not to hurry.
Nothing good gets away.

~ John Steinbeck

Look on every exit
as being
an entrance
somewhere else.

~ Tom Stoppard

There are two ways of spreading light;
to be the candle
or to be the mirror that reflects it.

~ Edith Wharton

I don't think of all the misery,
but of the beauty that
still remains.

~ Anne Frank

DAY 159

We are as much as we see.
Faith is sight and knowledge.
The hands only serve the eyes.

~ Henry David Thoreau

DAY *160*

When you focus on
the goodness in your life,
you create more of it.

~ Oprah Winfrey

You have been criticizing yourself
for years and it hasn't worked.
Try approving of yourself and
see what happens.

~ Louise L. Hay

DAY *162*

The most beautiful thing we can experience
is the mysterious.
It is the source of all true art and science.

~ Albert Einstein

DAY *163*

If you desire faith
then you have faith enough.

~ Robert Browning

DAY *164*

The best and most beautiful things
in the world cannot be seen or even touched—
they must be felt with the heart.

~ Helen Keller

Believe that life is worth living,
and your belief will help create
the fact.

~ William James

DAY *166*

That's the way
things become clear.
All of a sudden.
And then you realize
how obvious
they've been
all along.

~ Madeleine L'Engle

More things are wrought by prayer than this world dreams of.

~ Alfred, Lord Tennyson

Faith is not something to grasp;
it is a state to grow into.

~ Mohandas Gandhi

Love is
an act of faith,
and whoever is
of little faith
is also
of little love.

~ Erich Fromm

You must learn to be still
in the midst of activity
and to be vibrantly alive in repose.

~ Indira Gandhi

You must not abandon the ship in a storm
because you cannot control the winds.
What you cannot turn to good, you must
at least make as little bad as you can.

~ Thomas More

Gratitude
is the fairest
blossom
from which
springs
the soul.

~ Henry Ward Beecher

When we do
the best that we can,
we never know what miracle
is wrought in our life,
or in the life of another.

~ Helen Keller

Be faithful in small things—
because it is in them
that your strength lies.

~ Mother Teresa

It is better to light a candle
than curse the darkness.

~ Adlai Stevenson

Anything that is of value in life only multiplies when it is given.

~ Deepak Chopra

DAY *177*

Peace is always beautiful.

~ Walt Whitman

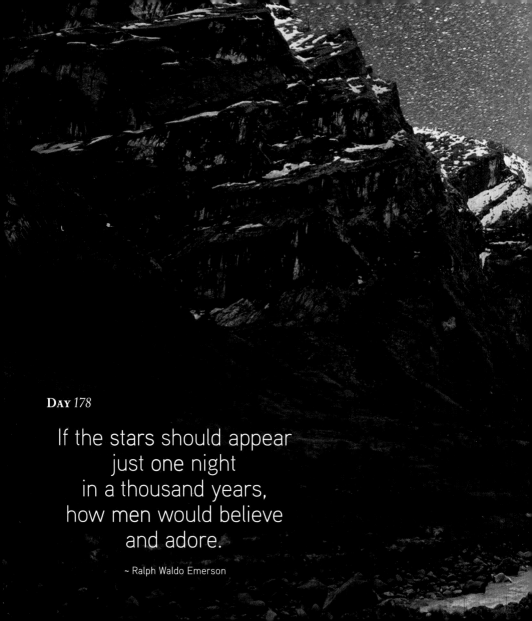

Day *178*

If the stars should appear
just one night
in a thousand years,
how men would believe
and adore.

~ Ralph Waldo Emerson

I say,
follow your bliss
and don't be afraid,
and doors
will open
where you
didn't know they
were going to be.

~ Joseph Campbell

CONTRIBUTOR INDEX

G

Galsworthy, John, *1867–1933*. British novelist and playwright.

Gandhi, Indira, *1917–1984*. Indian prime minister and politician.

Gandhi, Mohandas Karamchand (Mahatma), *1869–1948*. Indian civil rights leader.

Gibran, Kahlil, *1883–1931*. Lebanese-American artist, poet, writer, and philosopher.

Goethe, Johann Wolfgang von, *1749–1832*. German novelist, poet, playwright, and philosopher.

Graham, Martha, *1893–1991*. American modern dancer and choreographer.

H

Hay, Louise L., *b. 1926*. American motivational writer and publisher.

Hepburn, Katharine, *1907–2003*. American actress.

Hurston, Zora Neale, *1891–1960*. American novelist, essayist, and folklorist.

J

James, William, *1842–1910*. American psychologist and philosopher.

Jobs, Steve, *1955–2011*. American businessman, innovator, and entrepreneur.

Johnson, Samuel, *1709–1784*. British poet, essayist, literary critic, and lexicographer.

Jonson, Ben, *1572–1637*. British playwright, poet, and actor.

Jung, Carl (Gustav), *1875–1961*. Swiss psychiatrist and founder of analytical psychology.

K

Keller, Helen, *1880–1968*. American writer, lecturer, and activist.

Koller, Alice, *b. 1925*. American writer and scholar.

Kübler-Ross, Elisabeth, *1926–2004*. Swiss-American psychiatrist and pioneer in near-death studies.

L

Landers, Ann (Esther Lederer), *1918–2002*. American advice columnist and journalist.

Lao-tzu, *604–531 b.c.* Chinese philosopher.

La Rochefoucauld, François de, *1613–1680*. French memoirist and writer.

Lee, Harper, *b. 1926*. American novelist.

Le Guin, Ursula K., *b. 1929*. American novelist, poet, essayist.

Lenclos, Ninon de (Anne), *1620–1705*. French courtesan and author.

L'Engle, Madeleine, *1918–2007*. American novelist.

Lindbergh, Anne Morrow, *1906–2001*. American writer, poet, and aviator.

M

Macdonald, George, *1824–1905*. Scottish novelist, poet, and minister.

Miller, Henry, *1891–1980*. American novelist.

More, Thomas, *1478–1535*. English philosopher, statesman, and humanist.

Muir, John, *1838–1914*. Scottish American naturalist, author, and activist.

Murdoch, Iris, *1919–1999*. British novelist and philosopher.

N

Nash, Ogden, *1902–1971*. American poet.

Niebuhr, Reinhold, *1892–1971*. American theologian, author, and commentator.

Nin, Anaïs, *1903–1977*. French diarist and novelist.

O

Ortega y Gasset, José, *1883–1955*. Spanish philosopher and essayist.

P

Paine, Thomas, *1737–1809*. British pamphleteer, intellectual, and revolutionary.

Plutarch, *a.d. 46–120*. Greek historian.

Proust, Marcel, *1871–1922*. French novelist.

R

Rilke, Rainer Maria, *1875–1926*. Bohemian-Austrian poet.

Rodin, Auguste, *1840–1917*. French sculptor.

Roosevelt, (Anna) Eleanor, *1884–1962*. American First Lady, activist, and author.

Rosseau, Jean-Jacques, *1712–1778*. Swiss philosopher and writer.

Rowling, J. K. (Joanne Kathleen), *b. 1965*. British novelist.

Rumi (Jalal ad-Din ar-Rumi), *1207–1273*. Persian poet.

Russell, Bertrand, *1872–1970*. British philosopher, mathematician, and social critic.

S

Saint-Exupéry, Antoine de, *1900–1944*. French author, poet, and aviator.

Seneca, Lucius Annaeus, *4 b.c.–a.d. 65*. Roman philosopher, statesman, and dramatist.

Shakespeare, William, *1564–1616.* British playwright and poet.

Shaw, George Bernard, *1856–1950.* Irish playwright.

Sheehy, Gail, *b. 1937.* American journalist and author.

Smith, Betty, *1904–1972.* American novelist.

Spock, Benjamin, *1903–1998.* American pediatrician and author.

Steinbeck, John, *1902–1968.* American novelist.

Stevenson, Adlai, *1835–1914.* American politician and diplomat.

Stoppard, Tom, *b. 1937.* British playwright and screenwriter.

T

Tennyson, Alfred, Lord, *1809–1892.* British poet.

Teresa, Mother (Agnes Gonxha Bojaxhiu), *1910–1997.* Albanian-Indian nun and religious leader.

Thoreau, Henry David, *1817–1862.* American author, poet, and philosopher.

Tolle, Eckhart, *b. 1948.* German spiritual teacher and writer.

Tolstoy, Leo, *1828–1910.* Russian novelist and short story writer.

Tubman, Harriet, *1820–1913.* American abolitionist, humanitarian, and suffragist.

Tutu, Desmond, *b. 1931.* South African religious leader and antiapartheid activist.

Twain, Mark (Samuel Langhorne Clemens), *1835–1910.* American novelist and humorist.

U

Updike, John, *1932–2009.* American novelist, poet, and critic.

V

Virgil (Publius Vergilius Maro), *70–19 b.c.* Roman poet.

W

Walker, Alice, *b. 1944.* American novelist, poet, and activist.

Ward, William Arthur, *1921–1994.* American inspirational writer and poet.

Washington, Booker T., *1856–1915.* American educator, activist, author, and political leader.

Wharton, Edith (Newbold Jones), *1862–1937.* American novelist.

Whitman, Walt, *1819–1892.* American poet, essayist, and journalist.

Wilde, Oscar, *1854–1900.* Irish novelist and dramatist.

Williamson, Marianne, *b. 1952.* American spiritual writer and

poet.

Winfrey, Oprah, *b. 1954.* American media personality.

Woolf, Virginia (Adeline), *1882–1941.* British novelist and essayist.

Y

Yutang, Lin, *1895–1976.* Chinese novelist, essayist, and translator.

ILLUSTRATIONS CREDITS

If you have enjoyed this book
or it has touched your life in some way,
we would love to hear from you.

Please send your comments to:
Hallmark Book Feedback
P.O. Box 419034
Mail Drop 215
Kansas City, MO 64141

Or e-mail us at:
booknotes@hallmark.com